Photos of Ghosts

Poems by Gary Lechliter

Kansas City   Spartan Press   Missouri

Spartan Press
Kansas City, Missouri
spartanpresskc.com

Copyright (c) Gary Lechliter 2018
First Edition 1 3 5 7 9 10 8 6 4 2
ISBN: 978-1-946642-42-4
LCCN: 2018931381

Design, edits and layout: Jason Ryberg,
Cover art and design: Pam Lerow, Camille Lechliter
Title page image: Gary Lechliter
Author photo: Camille Lechliter
All rights reserved. No part of this publication may be reproduced or transmitted in any form or by any means, electronic or mechanical, including photocopying, recording or by info retrieval system, without prior written permission from the author.

Spartan Press would like to thank Prospero's Books, The Fellowship of N-finite Jest, The Prospero Institute of Disquieted P/o/e/t/i/c/s, Will Leathem, Tom Wayne, Jeanette Powers, j. d. tulloch, Jon Bidwell, Jason Preu, Mark McClane, Tony Hayden and the whole Osage Arts Community.

Sincere thanks to the following periodicals where these poems first appeared or are due to appear:

Chariton Review: "Photos of Ghosts," "The Fairy Ring," *Chiron Review:* "After the Birds," *Coal City Review:* "Banked Fires of Loved Ones," "Luck of the Draw," "The Things I've Seen"; *Cottonwood:* "After the Fall," *Haight Ashbury Review:* "The Recluse," *Main Street Rag:* "The Lost Poet," *Poem:* "End of November," *San Pedro River Review:* "After Shoveling Snow in the Dark," *Straylight:* "Tell God You're Still Visible," *Thorny Locust:* "Assuming That Existing Trends Continue," "Beautiful Bird," "Retirement Plans & Annuities," "The Day She Lost Her Keys." "Them Folks" and "Skidmore" appeared in *Give Me Your Lunch Money: Heartland Poets Speak out against Bullies."What Just Happened"* appeared in *Desolate Coutry: We the Poets, United, Against Trump.*

CONTENTS

The Day We Killed the Bull Snake / 1

Forty Acres / 3

The First Born / 5

Horsefly / 7

Banked Fires of Loved Ones / 8

After the Birds Are Gone / 10

Bur Oaks / 12

Rain / 14

End of November / 16

After Shoveling Snow in the Dark / 17

The Fairy Ring / 18

Road / 20

Beautiful Bird / 22

Luck of the Draw / 24

Skidmore / 26

Taking Her to Bed / 27

The Creation Museum / 28

Them Folks / 30

The Day She Forgets Her Purse / 31

The Bull Riders / 32

The Day She Lost Her Keys / 33

The Lost Poet / 34

The Recluse / 36

After the Fall / 37

In That State / 39

All the Stuff / 40

Some of my Brain / 41

All the Same / 42

The Things I've Seen / 43

Photos of Ghosts / 45

The Things We Gave to Goodwill / 46

Tomorrow / 48

Retirement Plans & Annuities / 49

Assuming That Existing Trends Continue / 50

To the Sky with Difficulty / 52

At Sixty-Five / 54

To The Highest Bidder / 55

What Just Happened? / 57

Unbridled / 59

Cognitive Dissonance of November 8th, 2016 / 61

Total Eclipse of the Sane / 62

If Only / 64

Nuclear Tulips / 65

Tell God You're Still Visible / 67

In memory of Ted and Joan Daldorph

The Day We Killed the Bull Snake

1959, Arkansas City, Kansas

I say we but it wasn't me. For
I was eight years old and had no say.
It was a lovely thing, that snake.
Five feet of muscle and scale.
And how I wanted to hold it,
just to get the feel of a creature
so intricately made, so deftly done.

But my mother saw it first and
screamed, as if the snake would
rise and strike me like a rattler,
as if my father would charge
from the house to be the hero,
and not the neighbor with his
cheap cigar and garden rake.

If a snake could scream, this one
would have, as it thrashed
and tried to coil, to right itself,
to somehow rearrange what
had been severed in haste
as the neighbor puffed his
stogie and beamed with pride.

And I stood there gazing at
the dying thing, tears held back,
words of protest unspoken.
Because kids should be seen
and not heard we were told.
Even when wrongs are done
by the taller children.

Forty Acres

for David

When my turn came I told the
class that we spent our family
vacation on the farm, where
grandfather's hayfork pitched
enough to fill the lofts, corn
snakes kept the rats at bay,
and cats worried the swallows.

We fed the pigs shelled corn,
and climbed the lowest limbs
of Winesap trees, small town
boys, tossing apples to the ground,
the ones that grandmother
sorted for pie and cobbler.

Early mornings my brother
sat on a three-legged stool
as grandfather filled the pails.
And because I'd spook the cows,
my chore was to gather eggs
with grandmother, whose
whispered song calmed the hens.

And naming the calves we liked
the most Ralph, Gene, or Becky,
we'd trail along toward dusk,
kicking cow-cakes in our path,
while grandfather called the herd
from the darkening fields.

The First Born

for my brother, David, 1950-2017

We lived in the same small clapboard house,
ate the same food, pissed in the same toilet,
bathed in the same old claw-foot tub.
We grimaced at the roaches and spiders
that shared our separate bedrooms.
And those nights when I could not sleep,
I heard the hard rail of your snoring.

By this I knew there were no ghosts.
It was just you, brother, that other kid,
the boy I barely knew, blown from the
same genes of our people. This is where
the story darkens, David, this is what
bounces around in my aging skull.

We were not brothers as brothers are
badged. Our lives did not entwine
with commonality, the caveat of same.
We were like boats on troubled seas,
each one sailing to opposite shores
with freight we carried to private ports.

Looking back at our lives, and now your
death, if you could you'd clap and agree
that no one's to blame for the wedge

between us that circumstance failed to move.
Maybe it was the religion you clung to,
that hard faith I walked away from,
the one you held to the dark end.

And I tell you with certainty that as the
Earth is fixed, it seems likely that I'll
see you soon, perhaps in some plausible
heaven for the faithful and, yes, the
agnostic, the Jew, the Buddhist and
Muslim, the gay or straight.

Horsefly

On wrongs swift vengeance waits.
                    -Alexander Pope

The fucker I smacked and left to die,
belly up on the ground, waits for
the labor of ants to carry it off.
It's not unlike the one that blooded
me as I played in my grandmother's
garden hose on a summer day.

That one made off with boy flesh.
And all I could do was weep and howl,
which brought my father out to the
lawn, where he chased it with the
newspaper's help wanted ads,
but could not smack the villain.

So now I must call this menace
I've flattened an icon of vengeance
and leave it in the mulch, where
the widow and fatherless grubs
will come to honor the knowledge
that only fools linger.

Banked Fires of Loved Ones

I am rowing, I am rowing
though the oarlocks stick and are rusty

—Anne Sexton, from *Rowing*

When I pay the coin
he helps me aboard
with weathered hands
and makes a place
for me by the oars.

If I say I'm weary
of the creak and heave,
the constancy of pull,
he offers me the tiller
for another coin,
or a cheater's game
of Five-card Draw.

We go on all night
crossing the Styx,
leaving my love to sleep
peaceful in her quilt
as we cut our sure
path on the water.

Charon says he knows
after all these years
the skin of the river,
cutbank and driftwood,
the clutter of moss.

Gulls unfamiliar to me
churn their calls on
the opposite shore.
And I long to dock
where the banked fires
of loved ones blaze.

Where my father
fishes for bullhead.
Where my mother
at last finds comfort
in the flame that warms
but will not burn.

After the Birds Are Gone

You wake up to a dismal
Earth that sadly lacks
the charm of chat and churr.
You miss the woodwind
of mourning doves,
whippoorwill in the woods,
the query of great horned owl.

Nothing hops through
your grass in search
of one good worm or seed.
No fledgling cries on
the ground for its mother.
No neighborhood cat stirs
its paw to grasp at ghosts.

You wonder if there isn't
one bald eagle, hawk
or falcon that survived.
You try to recall the wren,
high-tailed and fearless,
or the vanity and aplomb
of any male cardinal.

The woods stand bare
and barkless, where
beetles work their etchings.
Where the ornithologists
and birders no longer hold
awe for wings that push
the envelope of sky.

Bur Oaks

The winter trees, glazed with ice,
sleep with one dark eye open,
because they fear the lumberjack
and the axman, who deal with
need of fire in the hearth.

In spring the trees are dressed
for church in their Easter bloom,
proudly sprouting around town
pink and white, forsythia yellow,
the hues of hope for renewal.

Summer trees plump with birds
and shade for the neighbors, who
mow their lawns in the heat of day,
who weed their flowerbeds and mop
their brows, wishing for Fall.

And the autumn trees? O please!
The reds, the golds, the clatter.
The burning leaves. The calcium.
Children laughing in raked piles
where dogs wallow and piss.

But while most trees are gentle souls,
it's the ones that you've feared
for years you have to watch out for.
Like the angry elm on the corner
that trips you up in its roots.

That catalpa that drops beans
on your head, when you stroll
beneath the muffled laughter.
It's the hedge trees that spread
their warty balls in your path.

It's the locusts with thorny agendas.
Or the birch that scratches your
window at night, when the wind stirs.
And the worst you ask? Those
that list, all bent and gnarled.

The naked, haunted stumps
you drive past on freeways at
night, those that cross the lanes
with difficulty, like old men
in the brain's dissolve.

Rain

You can hear each drop hit the roof
and plink in the rainspout.
It's been three days of gray attitude
and fog settled in for the show.
Our dog won't piss outside in this soup.
Holding her bladder, she waits for
clearing and whines by the door.

The birds don't seem to mind it much.
With occasional shake and fluff they
continue the work of snatch and peck,
worm, seed, gruel for their young.
Sparrows keep vigil for the squirrels
and crows, those jackanapes that will
rob enough to assuage the chill.

All the trees guzzle like drunks.
Especially our birch, her trunk laid bare
from winter's loss that skinned her knees.
The redbuds flaunt more brown than red,
which is not what they're keen to do.
And in this weather who knows what
else the gods have for amusement.

We sometimes find it hard to believe
in weather like this, but it could be worse.
Like thunder overhead that rattles
the teeth, lightning striking so close
you swear your bones will chalk,
like the dead rising from graves
they'd rather not drown in.

End of November

We've done the requisites,
sent the last leaves to the dump
or burned them with risk.
We've cheered for calcium,
the cool, crisp air, and feasted
with thanks for the belly.

Or we've walked a dirt road.
Not that we need to, it goes with
the land, props up the scene,
whispers that we've walked a road
like that one before, those nights
we held somebody's hand.

Or we stood in the bleachers
and watched the marching
bands pass by, their uniforms
cut keen, drumbeats that
honed their quick steps
as the players took the field.

Now we see the ghost of hope
that stirs our winter's slurry,
and snow, the first to fall, so null
we sleep like the dead in rooms
of the soul, the blinds drawn,
the moon fogged and lost.

After Shoveling Snow in the Dark

I have decided not to die
in the driveway, slumped
in snow that fell on the sly
while everybody slept.

Who wants to die like that?
We want to die in our houses,
surrounded by loved ones
attending to our bedpans.

Nobody wants to kick-0ff
shoveling snow in the dark.
To die like that brings loss
that troubles the crows.

And even the lovers of winter
agree it's best not to die
in darkness like an idiot
as the snowplows roar.

The Fairy Ring

Amazed, I drop everything
to stand and stare in praise
for the ingenuity of earth.
I ponder how mushrooms
work the pattern in a circle,
and not square or rhomboid.

I crawl on my knees in the
morning grass, wet with dew,
to search for the blueprints
left behind by elfin engineers,
but find only hardhats and
slide rules tossed in a hurry.

Maybe they ran when my
face loomed huge and terrible.
Surely they thought some
warm-blooded Godzilla
would trash their architecture,
and they prayed for luck.

And now I am saddened
by the awkward intrusion,
for I mean them the least
harm of anyone who wants
to measure what cannot
be plucked for eating.

Their absence accuses me
of nothing I've done
to the monuments of mold
and spore, which call me
to weep and roll in the grass,
where some dog pissed.

Road

If, where fire and smoke are thickest, there's no work for you to do...

—Ellen M.H. Gates, 1860

Take this narrow dirt road,
wheels rattled on the cattle-guard,
past the creosote fence-posts
lit by low angles of the sun.
Drive past the aged bales, once
round, shagged and wooly.

Take this winding backroad
because you know it endures,
because the local grader pushed
rocks to brace your wheels
from the far side of the ditch,
holes from years of combines
and trucks to haul the corn.

Take this washboard road
with your window down to the
wind and leaves that catch your
face unaware, that wing their
flight like birds, hitchhiking
under your windshield wipers.

Take this one-horse road
and don't care a thing about it,
because it holds sure passage
where spent leaves cast their
fire and smoke, dust of ash,
hard winter coming.

Beautiful Bird

for Emily Sander

A towhee scratches drifts
in the carpet of spent leaves,
as a blade of sunlight angles
through cluttered woods,
where nothing nominates
the moment as new or strange.

Not even the image of a girl
now gone, or knowledge
that the weight of decisions
we sometimes make from need
stirs things that matter
in the broth of consequence.

No one here accuses her
or points a finger at disgrace,
because the jury of trees
serves no verdict of blame.
Because a choir of crickets
scratch their dirge for Emily,

because there is no one
who stands in the bluestem
to ponder what was right
and what was not, to count
guilt as so many words that
wedge in the throat like bones.

And now the towhee flies.
The sunlight dims with clouds
to usher the morning rain.
The leaves continue their
slow decay that brews mulch
where the crickets feed.

Luck of the Draw

for Jenny

I have not tried to rebuild
you, to pull you from the clay
in which you've slept these
forty-seven years, to work
the flesh and veins, the blood
and hair back to your bones.

But I have tried hard to learn
the everyday physics of life,
to ponder what went wrong,
how a gun could hit the
floor and discharge, how
the bullet found your brain.

And none of it makes sense
in the plausible world.
Not the angle of trajectory.
The damn luck of the draw.
The absence of angels to pull
you from the line of fire.

I would not remold you as
I knew you, the girl I had
no chance of holding, who
spoke with me as the boy
lost in the social graces,
that sat next to her in class.

Jenny, I will not claim to
have loved you, fleeting,
as adolescents do, that we
shared anything near to love,
or that we could, in the
short run, ever wallow

in the temporal nonsense
of teenage attraction
to youth, beauty and touch,
changeable as the wind.
So Jenny, I must hold you
in the coils of memory

and go on as I have for
five decades, to question
the ability to forget you
and the place where you
lie, the grave forgotten,
but not the loss.

Skidmore

A pall from the coffin seems to
linger here, even after thirty-five years.
Bricks hold a trace of it — with the
image of the nameless face,
the hero who rid the town of a bully
so vile that even the local sheriff
had no office when called for.

It's a long time between beers
and piss, and the townsfolk go
on as they must with farming
and drug stores, children at the
bus stop, the honored stories of
the bully's kids, ten in all, lost
mothers of forsaken breasts.

And even today the town's name
calls questions of guilt or relief,
as those who remember walk back
the logic that the needs of many
outweigh the ignorance of one.
That the law's a fluid, pliant thing
if the end justifies the blood.

Taking Her to Bed

As we step through the front door,
the milieu of the house is dark
and empty. Shadows shrink to
the corners, the freezer chugs-out ice.
Dust-balls roll like tumbleweeds,
gathering evidence of neglect.

She gives me one of those looks —
her gentle eyes reflecting trust,
the prescient tongue swaying,
as I hang up my jacket and hat.
It's time to go to bed she says,
without speaking a word.

And what can I do but agree?
What else can I have but the
joy of her body firm in my arms,
as I carry her to the still warm
bed, where she licks my nose
and pants like a lover.

The Creation Museum
Petersburg, Kentucky

Learn from yesterday, live for today, hope for tomorrow.
The important thing is not to stop questioning. —Albert Einstein

Here they speak of truth, labeled,
packaged for the masses, shrink-
wrapped and printed, stacked
for immediate consumption
by children, wide-eyed, hungry.

Displays tell of dinosaurs and
men, Velociraptor in the Garden,
T. Rex keen for lunch of greens,
those terrible teeth ripping
through Brussels sprouts.

Signs proclaim science wrong,
the Earth not measured by
billions, but younger than the
Neanderthals, who grunted their
last breaths forty thousand years ago.

Here six-day creation cannot
be framed as a factor, no way
to test the premise, no null
to be rejected, no results
verified with statistical analysis.

And because the only error
is doubt, and doubt can't
be allowed, nothing's more
cute than unquestionable faith
in six thousand years of chaos.

Them Folks

We sometimes wander the landscapes
of people we badge as odd or strange
because the difference scares us.
Like the judge who paces his backyard.
The girl who won't go outside her
house or to rooms with a crowd.

The lovely boy who's lonely and gay,
and knows he will never marry in Kansas.
The *Hat Woman* who stands at the
curb to advise them folks where
salvation's found, who they must serve,
and can they spare some change?

There's the man who's afraid of rain,
who finds it hard to make sense
of it all, to hold reason in the darkest day,
when he draws the blinds and
prays for drought, as the clouds
spill enough to cleanse the town.

And it's fear that no one's the same
that moves the neighborhood bully
to loose his dog to frighten passersby,
the neighbors and the postman,
the sellers of faith and magazines,
because they're different.

The Day She Forgets Her Purse
for Susie

On this Tuesday of winter fog,
with Christmas just up the road,
she has forgotten her purse,
the dark brown one with the
leather shoulder strap, pockets
and snaps to keep it together.

There's a picture of the dog she lost
to age, the miniature schnauzer,
and the one that remains that
will surely die soon. That snapshot
she carries must be one of her daughter
who's lived next-door for years.

The office keys that keep things
moving along, that jangle
in her hands when she walks
into the office, also gone.
Those tactile things she needs,
the small objects and baubles.

These are the stuff that matter
eight hours a day, five days a week,
the cogs that drive inertia.
And without them there's undoing,
like the absence of old dear friends
or the cage without its finch.

The Bull Riders

Under the lasers and replay screen,
the cowboys walk out all fringe and leather.
They've come to the Kansas Expocentre,
prepared to be maimed and mashed,
to risk getting snagged in the riggings.

Possibility of death or broken neck,
hitch-to-the-get-along for the rest of their lives.
But they know the fearsome odds
and gamble those young, athletic
bodies for our amusement.

I certainly would not trade places
with them or the bulls, the other heroes:
Fast Eddie, Cujo, Shotgun Red.
So much heart in spurious spins,
high, stiff kicks, the bestial blaze.

And behind the bent-pipe barriers,
I try to imagine just how much
hard cash it would take to get
this already banged-up body bucked
in less than eight seconds.

The Day She Lost Her Keys
for Jill

was the day nothing worked.
The morning was defective.
The coffee tasted like swill.
Everyone in the office searched
and came up empty-handed.
Paper clips, hidden for years,
were freed from the cobwebs—
and still the keys were lost.

Chance, strongly off kilter,
ridged on theories of luck.
The ordinary air of Tuesday
grew mealy and crabbed.
Printers chugged-out nothing.
Mice giggled from their holes.
Everything we never believed
became exceedingly clear.

Meanwhile, the lesser angels,
who didn't want to get involved,
sat and twiddled their thumbs.
The gods kept hitting the booze.
Hope rolled over and whined.
And the gremlins rallied
to praise their endless work
of lousing things up.

The Lost Poet

for James Tate (1943–2015)

We have not tried to find you
anymore, and perhaps that's
how you like it. Perhaps you saw
us dredge the river and you wanted
to shout, *I'm Ok, I'm over here.*
Perhaps you did and we could not
hear you for the hum of traffic.

And because we love you we were
dedicated to search every coffee dive
with a microphone and a stool.
We had the whole thing planned out,
a mob of volunteers on a rescue
of enormous proportions.
And still we could not find you.

Because it was difficult at first
to think of giving up, because we
hoped that we'd run across you
gathering wool in the only bookstore
on Main Street, where we thought
you'd peruse the dusty shelves
for all your remaindered books.

But no one has seen you gad
around, leaning like a tramp
on the flagpole, our only compass.
Where anyone passing through
could find their way by turning
right or left or going straight
to nowhere in particular.

The Recluse

They say that God is everywhere, and yet we always think of Him as somewhat of a recluse. —Emily Dickinson

I have not seen her in all the
strolls I've taken past her place,
where the stems of weed and
timothy are tall enough to bale.

What she knows and who she
loved is the stuff of quandary,
her face unseen, voice only heard by
boys who deliver the groceries.

She might have a car in the garage,
but no one says they've seen it
parked in the crumbled driveway
or driven through the town.

And after all, perhaps she's pleased
for the worn house to be haunted
by any shroud or bone that holds
the comfort of solitude.

After the Fall

Semimaru, blind in your refuge,
where you strummed the moon's 4 strings,
what came of them, in the long run,
the notes so keen and lunar?

Having seen darkness from the cliff
that ridges on death, I know the light
of recovery room, the overhung lamps.
The fog of nurse and tech, doctors in
their godlike certainties, the saline drip
and the saline drip, boots that walk past
a window where there is no window.

Having visited the abyss, though
brief, and returned to my place in the
queue, I treasure the red and lapis
lazuli of dawn, the transient hues.

Having been near soulless, bereft
of thought, then snapped back to life,
even the workdays, tedious, needful,
stand as surrogates for the lack
of light and of being, factors that
surely make their play for nothing
but indefatigable ends.

What I'm saying is I've been lucky,
a sinistral klutz who should be
hugging the slab by now, who
would be known as the lesser and
least of a species called poet.

What I'm saying is nothing's new.
That Memory strips naked and jogs
past every night, wagging her nipples,
that the ghosts of lost verse wander on
streets most luminous, hands in pockets,
searching for newborn poems.

In That State
(after the fall)

How long I was out I don't recall.
From the ground to the trauma ward
I slept long and flirted with death.
And did I dream or catch a glimpse
of Heaven, Hell, or Purgatory?

If I did I don't remember, if I did
I never wrote it down, never called
it a book, or toured the country
to scribble my name on the covers.

Invitations to speak in multi-million
dollar stadiums never happened.
I just woke up and looked around
at all the machines and devices
that kept me broken but alive.

In that state facts were irrational.
I didn't know a damned thing
about the fall, who was at fault,
what the angels said about it.

I only knew the beige curtains,
the tired nurses and technicians,
doctors with grim assignments,
the tubes funneling needful fluid
through arteries and veins.

All the Stuff

The spidery darkness of corners.
Nurses rolling carts down the hall.
Whispered invectives of concern.
With footsteps quick and deliberate,
smiles pasted on, they move with the
rhythm of ants searching for crumbs.

Any empty bags I'm attached to
are taken down and tossed away.
There's something called depression
that I've learned so much about,
the effects of all the stuff they've
jammed in the tangle of veins.

And here I lie all cold and clammy,
like some rotten skunk on the road,
while Death plays poker with God.
A small boy, feeling sorry for myself,
I hold the dark history of my skull,
busted like a kid's piggy bank.

Some of my Brain
I like nonsense; it wakes up the brain cells. —Dr. Seuss

Some of my brain was scraped away
to save what remained of the whole,
stirred by the fall, a skull full of jelly,
the remnants of pia matter,
all the brickwork that holds the self.

Some of my brain and the gravy
of blood were removed and tossed.
And that part of me, though miniscule,
can't regenerate like a skink's tail,
because it's the only model of its kind,
the form and gestalt of my birth.

Some of my brain misses what's lost.
And how can it function like it used to?
How can the aging lobes recall with clarity
the schools and factors I was taught:

Freud's Id, Ego, Super Ego, Jung's Archetypes,
the study of the individual in groups,
theories of personality and motivation,
the drive to get up and eat.

All the Same

I travel home like a man
lost to whatever happened
before the fall. It's October,
the air crisp, the scent
of rot drifting through the
car window, as my wife
drives those silent miles.

The motley trees we pass
in the fields and farms,
the maples, oaks, birches,
sail their various hues,
like nothing has changed
to alter the landscape
of backroads and corn.

We pull in the driveway
beside the spent petunias
and untrimmed yews,
a dark stain on the place.
And Jesus Christ, there's
the very place where I fell
and the brain bled out.

The Things I've Seen

There's this thing outside
our window, not unlike the
one I saw last night, about
the size of a runway model,
gaunt and tall like a stork.
It might be the neighbor's
thing that escaped from

their backyard and slipped
through the fence slats.
Possibilities abound for
a thing like that, full to the
brim with history of all
the things I've seen.

Like the one that knocked
on our door, sometime
in the 1950s, the winter
of angry sky, hoarfrost
on spillways to the river,
snowmen that held onto
each other for warmth.

Things often slept on our
hide-a-bed until the snow
drifts waned to puddles,
the tulips were done with
pink, and the dandelions
spread their loose heads.

But one wild thing partied
late and vexed my mother,
who trundled from bed
at 3:00 in the morning
to let it in, as it drunkenly
fell to the living room floor
beside the Motorola.

Photos of Ghosts

for Charles Simic

Come back tonight in the snow.
You left your watch and fly swatter
by the kitchen sink, where flies
swarm above the dishwater, those
bad guests of winter, inside for soup
and crackers to warm the gut.

Come back to the pantry with your
can-opener, or we'll surely faint from
hunger, and not be ourselves for days.
Stand by the table that was given
to us those decades ago, when
our love and the house was new.

You're barely gone and you miss
me still. What's it been 10 seconds?
Your hat and coat hang dusty
in the hall like you never left.
And all the mirrors, with photographs
of ghosts, hold no image of you.

The Things We Gave to Goodwill

Our history went out the door,
most of it dusty and worn,
like the Christmas ornaments
we once treasured, those that will
hang like new on someone's tree.

Clothing we cannot wear now,
the business suits and a few ties,
an overcoat shouldered in dust,
black dress shoes worn at the
heels, all the articles of work.

Some toys the grandkids have
outgrown, the ones they enjoyed,
will sit on the shelves where
kids grab them and love them
until they've grown dark.

Books by the dozen, fiction,
paperbacks, murder mysteries,
travel guides to where we've
been, magazines, anthologies,
all to be read or recycled.

Some things we nearly kept
because they hold memories,
the horse blanket we huddled
in that winter we watched
eagles perch at the lake,

the china and punchbowls
that were new when our
dining room table was new,
the ceramic desk lamp, a gift
from an aunt long gone.

And to this charity we gave
our stuff, the old knickknacks
that show how we've tried
with the imperative of aging
to sweep the new in.

Tomorrow

I will get out of bed with the birds
and walk out the kitchen door to the deck
in my stocking feet, barely dressed.
My willowy hair will entertain cowlicks.
Frost will call from the long grass.

Neighborhood cats will scrap in the brush.
The muse that crawls from a manhole
will wander around like a notion.
And I will ponder, with coffee cup in
hand, the aging brain with its wisdom.

Then I will preach like I used to do.
There will be a congregation of ghosts
robed in old sheets from Goodwill.
There will be an avian choir with arias,
the first soprano a dark-eyed junco.

There will be wooly bears on the fence,
crows that barter for an onion ring,
the wind's augury of winter coming on,
squirrels barking their pious ownership
of every nut in the block.

Retirement Plans & Annuities

Rehearse the hands-on-chest position.
Eventually you'll look like yourself.
Take the dog out to pee and putz around
In your robe and house shoes,
Re-water the grass and pots, then revisit
Everything you did the day before.
Make sure you pick up the dog poop.
Empty the birdbath and refill it. When
Neighbors walk past, wave and nod at
The ones who retired before you.

Phone the authorities to report the
Lout who steals your morning paper
And the stray cat that kills the wrens,
Nuthatches and vireos you feed.
Stand like a statue in the long grass

& piss covertly on the clover.

After you read the AARP magazine,
Nothing new between the covers,
No famous codger's biography,
Unmoved, toss it to the bin
In the garage with the cardboard.
Then a nap after lunch from the
Indefatigable reality that nothing
Exciting to do every day
Sums the need to continue.

Assuming That Existing Trends Continue
*In response to the young man riding in the truck with
a bumper-sticker that reads "Jesus is the Answer"*

As engines idle at a stoplight,
a young man in the jacked-up
pickup hollers as he spits his
snuff: *You old weirdo.* Which
moves me to look around for
anyone else who might be
the object of adolescent tripe.

Instead I see there's only me
who wears the misfit badge.
The light turns and I drive on.
At 64 I don't need to complicate
the matter by responding to
his vitriol with my own reply:
Thanks very much, bigot.

And as I ponder the bumper
sticker, I'm prone to cry out,
What's the question? Are all
things Jesus if given specific
conditions of variability?
Does God change his socks?
Is faith more a concept?

But now I must concentrate
or I'll surely have a wreck,
and the officer will inform me
that if existing trends continue
I'll lose my driver's license,
rattle around like a walnut,
and worry the squirrels.

To the Sky with Difficulty

There is no one I recognize less than myself.
The glimpsed reflection in the mirror, computer
screen, downtown store window, all reminding
me of who I'm not and, at this age, the ghostly
face, the hair grown thin and reedy.

Reason enough not to keep the glasses
clean, to see through fog the old poet
in his dubious wisdom. It's like a horse
that grazes in fescue, put to pasture
and eventual dog food.

Weeks go by and each day presents as just a day.
What day this is, for example, I don't care.
I put the trash to the curb this morning.
And that means it's Wednesday, halfway
through the week, ridged on Thursday.

At this point in life the brain's house
crowds with squatters that call themselves
guests, memories camped in the living
room, where tent-poles pierce the ceiling
and bonfires of insomnia thin the air.

And because there's no faith I cling to anymore,
the angels in their quaint assignments
hang out in the neighbor's house,
the ones that go to church, praise the Lord
with gladness, love one another ideally.

Perhaps If I cut my hair I'd still not know
myself, when the locks of gray that cover
the vacancies of age lose their hold,
and the omnipresent Kansas winds
blow the cowlicks wild.

At Sixty-Five

I am becoming one of the old men.
>—James Wright, from *A Poem of Towers*

I refuse to be one of the old men!
And furthermore, I shun the use
of the cane and walking stick
that lean at the wall by the fireplace
in case the flames need feeding.

I refuse to be one of the old men!
Even though I'm part of their
gestalt, even though I get a discount
for hanging around a long time
with no good reason to leave.

To The Highest Bidder

What would you give for the ripe poet?
Do I hear a bid? Anyone? Anyone?
How much is the well-aged body worth?
How much the soul, the old ash of it?

Let's start the bidding at one paper dollar.
Anyone? Anyone? Just raise your hand.
Yes sir, you sir, I see your hand raised.
One dollar from Mr. William Lechliter.

That gives us one dollar, do I hear two?
Who'll give me two dollar, two dollar, who?
Dollar and a half, anyone, anyone?
You in the corner, I see your bid.

Dollar and a half from Laura Mae Lechliter.
Now two, now two, who'll give me two?
Two dollar, two dollar, who'll make it two
for this fine specimen of agnostic?

Surely there's someone who'll give me two.
Yes, I see you, two dollars from the dark
hooded figure in the back row. Now
three dollar, three dollar, three dollar.

Who'll give me three dollar, anyone?
Three dollar, three, who'll bid three?
Going, going, any more bids? Sold
for two dollars and no cents

What Just Happened?

*Understanding does not cure evil, but it is a definite help,
inasmuch as one can cope with a comprehensible darkness.*

—Carl Jung

We went to a movie as the polls closed,
needing anything to break the tension.
And now we cannot remember the title
or the plot, who played who, the ending.
Afterward we ate at our favorite café.
It all seemed normal, as it should be.
Surely, we said, our country will progress.

But when we returned home to watch
the votes roll in, hopeful for the future
of our grandchildren and their children,
we sat there stunned, like the world was
ending, like fate had sucker-punched us.
At that moment the Earth was off kilter.
At that moment gravity slipped a stitch.

The laws of physics were rendered null.
And maybe the Earth is truly a pancake,
not some chubby little orb we spin on.
Sense and responsibility packed their bags
and took the first flight to anywhere
that values the worth of the soul, that
loves the rare, sleek skin of difference.

The night and the solar shadow's idea
of the moon had rotted all its cheese.
There was a rustle among the ghosts.
The neighborhood gnomes wept and
pissed in their shoes, something moved
hard through the trees, the dry limbs
of cottonwood bending, breaking.

We knew that elections are rough-hewn,
and so we sobbed in the finest scotch
for what will occur the next four years,
and can't be corrected with regrets.
Our old bed cried to be slept on, and try
we did, thrashing like helpless carp
thrown on the bank to rot.

Unbridled

There is nothing more dangerous than the conscience of a bigot.
—George Bernard Shaw

In the past when we lost we felt no worse
than losing the World Series or the Super Bowl.
Wrong person in office, but we'd be OK.
We shook it off and went on with life.
In four years we'd try again.

But losing this time is like the moon
showing her dark side, the stars gone dull.
Dogs howling in the bleak winter,
and winter long, our breakfast gruel,
our better angels gone south.

Losing this time brings with it grudges,
families torn, friends drifted off,
social media a plague of chintzy, fake news.
Uncertainty of peace and the binding
and gagging of progress now the norm.

And Jesus Christ, we hear the dissonant
cry of the faithful, some blessed that
they voted for the Lord, leaving the truth
static, their religion hung on the rack
to dry like shit in the wind.

Now the ground of tolerance quakes
through backroads and streets.
And there'll be no joy for those who
bet their children on a dark horse,
the one that gallops wild.

Cognitive Dissonance of November 8th, 2016

There was a great shackling of thought
when nothing mattered but the
needs of those who blinded themselves to the future
of our country, the nobility of office.

Many were faithful believers
who suffered from the conflicts
of supporting what's immoral
for the sake of Jesus Christ,

or someone like the manufactured
image of Christ, pliable as you
like it, a transient guide,
made to order for any occasion.

Total Eclipse of the Sane

In all chaos there is a cosmos, in all disorder a secret order.
—Carl Jung

In the year of entropy after the election...

Just past daylight and where's your Mom?
Where's the god you wished for so long ago?
Who's that sobbing alone in their backyard?
Why should you care about your neighbor's grief?
She's the one who lost her way. She's the one
who hates the shiftless night-birds circling,
their beaks gathering luckless bugs.

2.
Funny, this darkness, you whisper to no one.
Isn't it odd how colors cut their hues to nil?
Jesus, she's still hunkered down by the fence,
and there's nothing you can do to assuage
her sorrow, without being some kind of jerk,
the one who can never leave it alone.

3.
It looks like rain off to the east of town
to the blind eye that sees such things.
A chorus of curs growls from the street,

where soggy french-fries spark a fight
over something insufficient to nourish
strays that no one gives a tick about.

4.
Around the neighborhood darkness fits
like a shroud in this part of town. Only
here and there the windows of bedrooms,
curtains drawn, the glimpse of blinds.
The shrill cry of a lost cat tempered
by something crashing through ancient
elms that were felled last Fall.

If Only

The poetry editors regret to inform
me, after a year has passed, that
they never received my submission,
the one I mailed on a snowy day.

Perhaps it ended up in the Maldives,
where the poems bask like tourists.
I'd like to think they miss being read,
if only to be laughed at, scorned.

And all of the poems recall what they
would have shown the editors, if only
they'd been given the chance, if only
the postman had done things right.

I picture one poem musing about
the gloom of winter, the drab hours,
snow that continues through the
night, dawn's roar of sand-trucks.

While the other poems recite their
verse and drool in their Daiquiris,
none of them longing to return
to America in her dark time.

Nuclear Tulips
for Barb

There was nothing I could do.
The wind was up and late for work.
The squirrel in the birdfeeder
hogged the needful seeds
and left the sparrows to riot.

There was nothing I could do
when the bulbs I planted last fall
rose, sprouted, bloomed
and mingled with the clutch
of luminous daffodils.

There was nothing I could do.
The new day cried in its diaper.
The retired streetwalker rode
past on her motorized cane,
waving like an idiot at a passerby.

There was nothing I could do
or say or write or feel or know
that made a lick of difference
in news gone viral on the internet
of climate change denial.

There was nothing I could do.
The mayonnaise farmers were out
of work, gefilte fish belly-up
in the river, and the God Particle
thirsted for heavy water.

Tell God You're Still Visible

after all these years of not being seen.
Walk around with your hands in plain sight.
Step carefully around mirrors.
Hang out at the shopping mall
to watch the people pass in unison,
all of them staring at three nude
women walking their poodles.

2.
Shoot a game of pool with yourself
and remember those disco years,
the dangled ball, enormous hats,
shoes with platform heels.
And the Whozits? What was the name
of that band, the one with scantily clad guys
gyrating under a blizzard of hair?

3.
Clap one hand like you mean it.
Follow a conclusion to its nest.
Stir the straw to fit your soul,
settling in for a long, dark winter
with the ghosts of gloom.
Let the abuse of religion you've
known since childhood keep you warm.

4.
You be the one to make it happen.
You clip the coupons and mail them in.
You tell God you're still visible
and wish her well in all the entanglements
of men that she must deal with.
You be the one that never overlooks
those hard to miss spots.

-- thanks to Ashley Davis

Gary Lechliter's work has recently appeared in many poetry journals and anthologies. He has published three full-length books of poetry. His newest book *Off the Beaten Path* is published by Woodley Press. Gary is the managing editor of *I-70 Review*.

This project was made possible, in part, by generous support from the Osage Arts Community.

Osage Arts Community provides temporary time, space and support for the creation of new artistic works in a retreat format, serving creative people of all kinds — visual artists, composers, poets, fiction and nonfiction writers. Located on a 152-acre farm in an isolated rural mountainside setting in Central Missouri and bordered by ¾ of a mile of the Gasconade River, OAC provides residencies to those working alone, as well as welcoming collaborative teams, offering living space and workspace in a country environment to emerging and mid-career artists. For more information, visit us at www.osageac.org

www.ingramcontent.com/pod-product-compliance
Lightning Source LLC
Chambersburg PA
CBHW021448080526
44588CB00009B/749